24 New Tunes in Common Meter

24 New Tunes in Common Meter

A Companion for the Psalter and Congregational Psalm Singing

Ran Whitley

Tampa, Florida

The content associated with this book is the sole work and responsibility of the author. Gatekeeper Press had no involvement in the generation of this content.

24 New Tunes in Common Meter: A Companion for the Psalter and Congregational Psalm Singing

Published by Gatekeeper Press
7853 Gunn Hwy., Suite 209
Tampa, FL 33626
www.GatekeeperPress.com

Copyright © 2024 by Ran Whitley
All rights reserved. Neither this book, nor any parts within it may be sold or reproduced in any form or by any electronic or mechanical means, including information storage and retrieval systems, without permission in writing from the author. The only exception is by a reviewer, who may quote short excerpts in a review.

The cover design and editorial work for this book are entirely the product of the author. Gatekeeper Press did not participate in and is not responsible for any aspect of these elements.

ISBN (paperback): 9781662949265

Foreword

The Book of Psalms is the Lord's revelation providing His people with substance for worship, lament, reflection, introspection, confession and praise. Accordingly, the Apostle Paul entreats us to sing psalms and hymns and spiritual songs. Yet what has happened to psalm singing in the modern church?

Most modern hymnals do contain a faint vestige of the Book of Psalms enduring from the *Genevan Psalter*. But how seriously does the modern church heed the scriptural admonition to sing psalms? And how can the modern church reclaim the rich treasure contained in the Psalter?

I deem the primary reason for resistance is the use of fatigued and dated hymn tunes most often utilized with psalter texts. The truth and authority of God's word does not change, but contemporary culture and musical style are everchanging. This tune collection, *24 New Tunes in Common Meter*, is composed to this end to assist churches in the reclamation of the rich theological treasure found in the Book of Psalms and the psalter.

Each new tune herein conforms to strophic common meter or common meter doubled.   The style is intentionally contemporary with a variety of interesting rhythms, harmonies, color tones, chord extensions and modalities not appearing in traditional hymn tunes. Each new tune is scored for gentle vocal range and easy piano accompaniment. Chord symbols have been provided to facilitate adaptation of rhythm instruments such as guitar, keyboard, bass and drums.

My prayer is that your church will find this collection of tunes useful in accessing and reclaiming the Book of Psalms in congregational worship.

Ran Whitley, DMin, PhD
Professor of Music
Campbell University

TABLE OF CONTENTS

Page	Tune Name	Meter	Key
1	Alpha	8.6.8.6.	C Major
2	Beta	8.6.8.6.	Bb Major
3	Gamma	8.6.8.6.	A Dorian
4	Delta	8.6.8.6.	C Mixolydian
5	Epsilon	8.6.8.6.	C Major
6	Zeta	8.6.8.6.	Bb Major
7	Eta	8.6.8.6.	G Major
8	Theta	8.6.8.6.	C Major
9	Iota *(in canon)*	8.6.8.6.	Eb Major
10	Kappa	8.6.8.6.	E Minor
11	Lambda	8.6.8.6.	C Pentatonic
12	Mu	8.6.8.6.D.	C Major
13	Nu	8.6.8.6.D.	F Major
14	Xi	8.6.8.6.D.	Eb Major
15	Omicron	8.6.8.6.D.	Bb Major
16	Pi	8.6.8.6.D.	G Major
17	Rho	8.6.8.6.D.	F Major
18	Sigma	8.6.8.6.D.	F Major
19	Tau	8.6.8.6.D.	C Major
20	Upsilon	8.6.8.6.D.	C Major
21	Phi	8.6.8.6.D.	F Major
22	Chi	8.6.8.6.D.	E Minor/G Major
23	Psi	8.6.8.6.D.	C Major
24	Omega	8.6.8.6.D.	F Major

PSALM ONE
Alpha (8.6.8.6.)

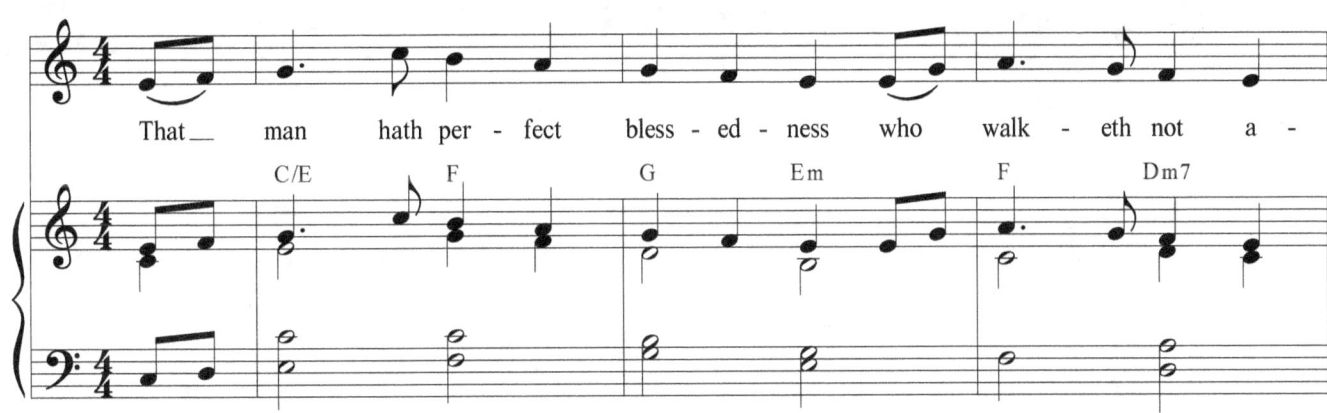

That man hath perfect blessedness who walketh not astray

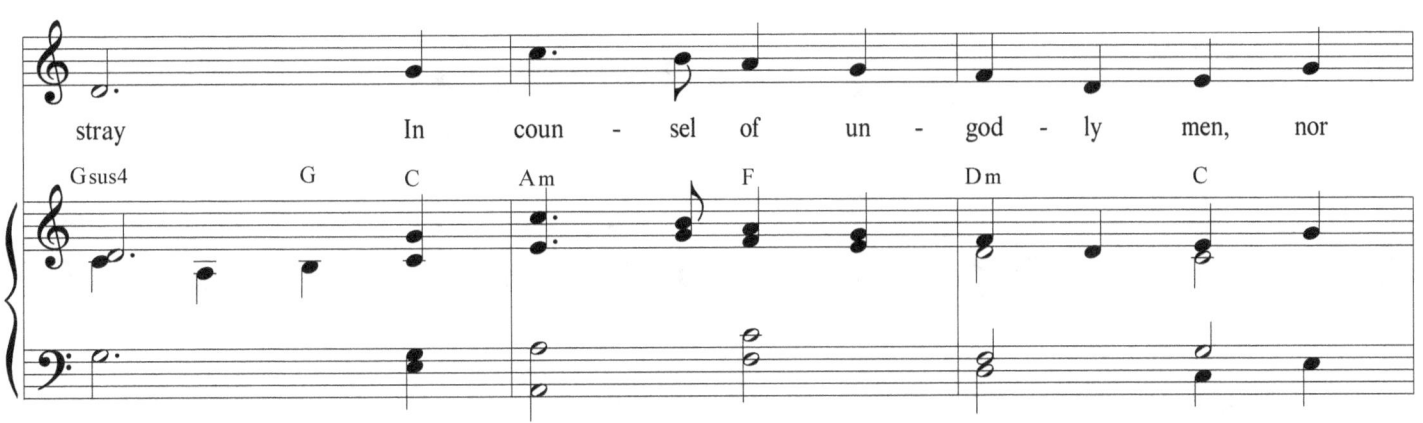

In counsel of ungodly men, nor

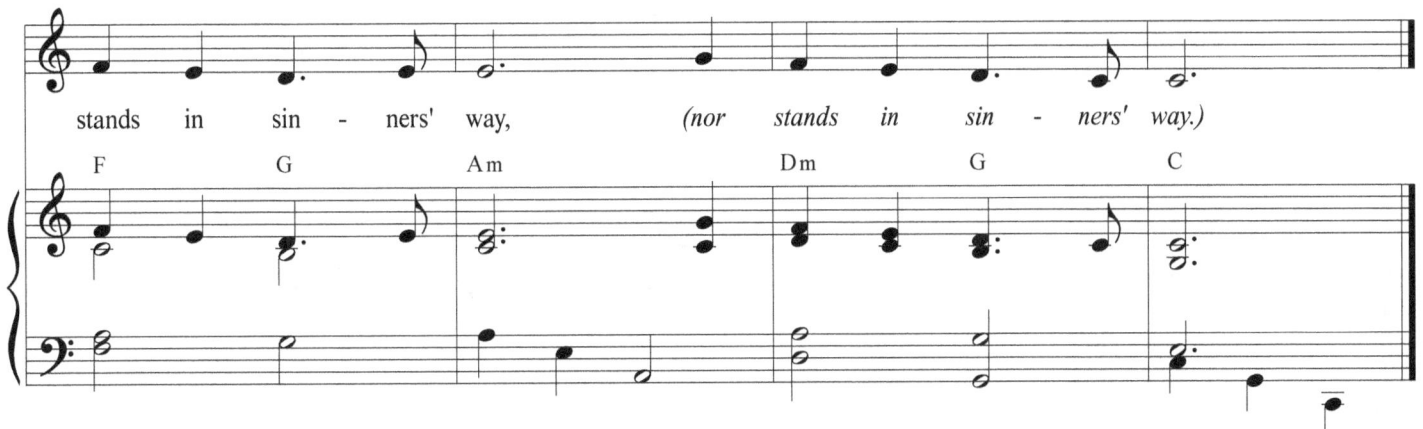

stands in sinners' way, (nor stands in sinners' way.)

PSALM ONE
Beta (8.6.8.6.)

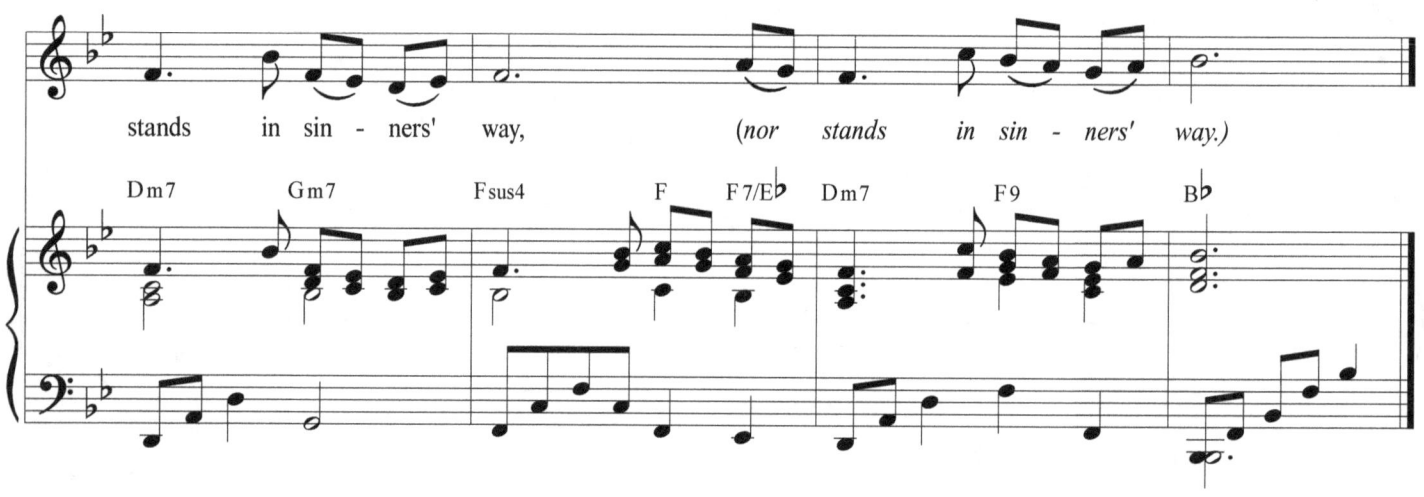

PSALM ONE

Gamma (8.6.8.6.)

PSALM ONE
Delta (8.6.8.6.)

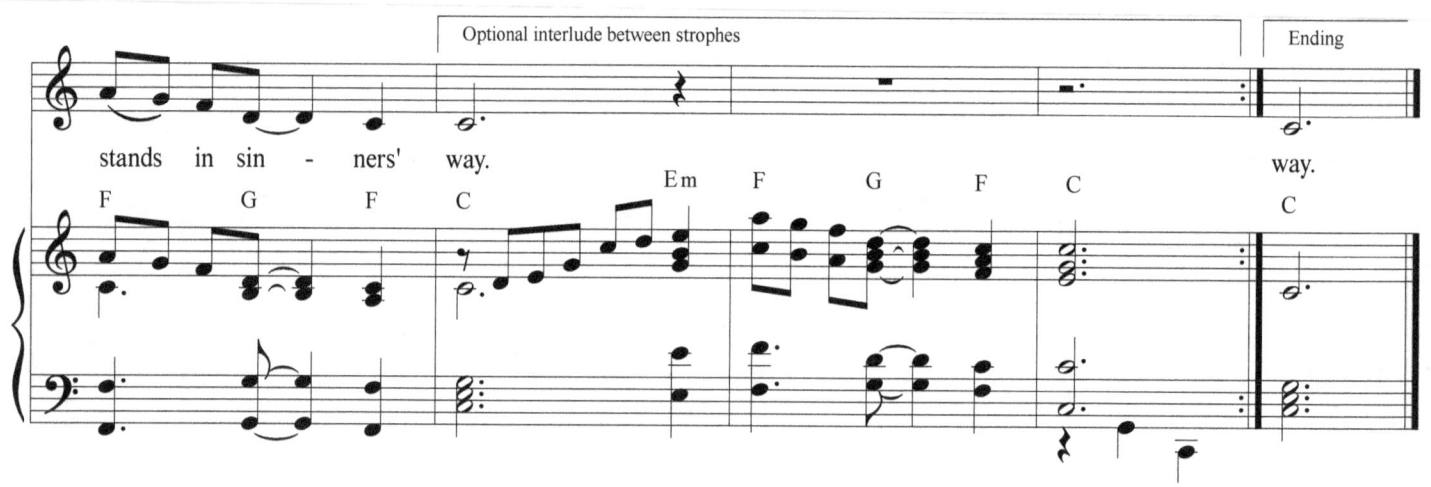

PSALM ONE
Epsilon (8.6.8.6.)

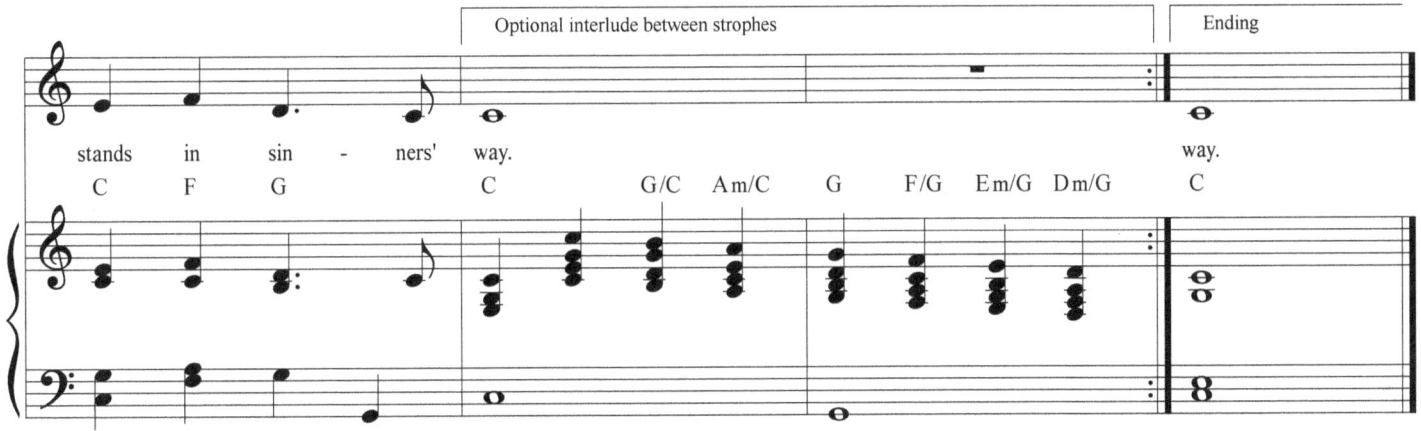

PSALM ONE
Zeta (8.6.8.6.)

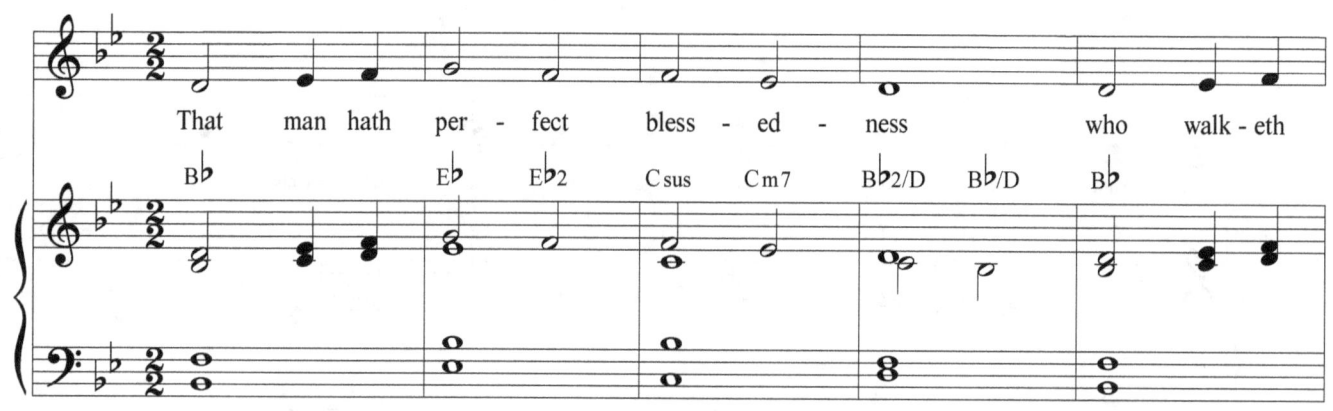

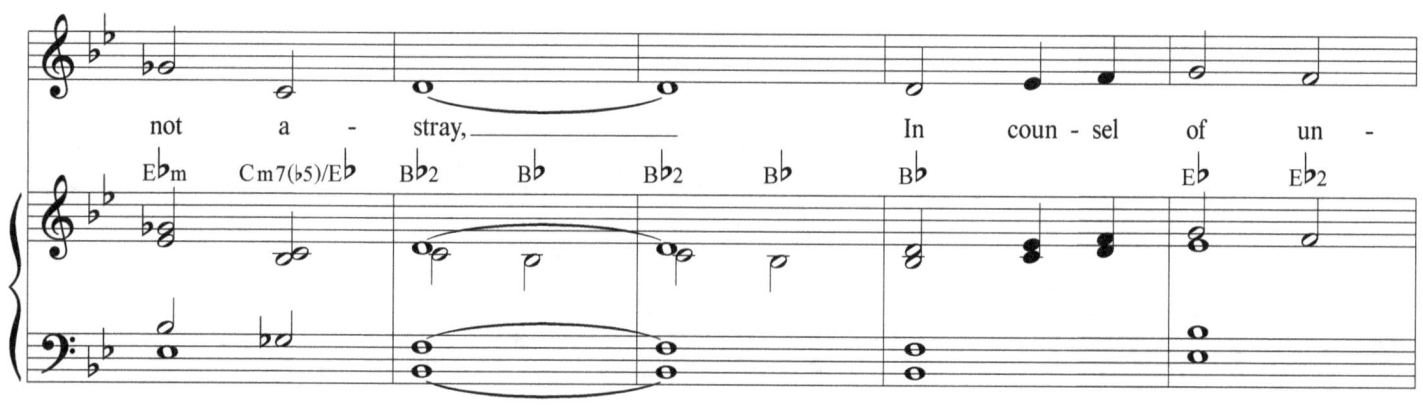

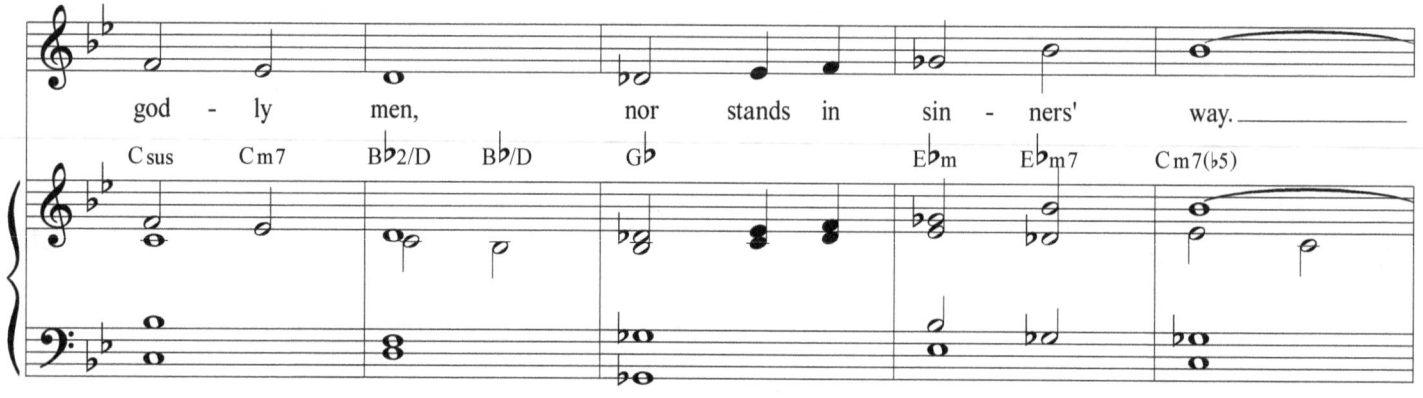

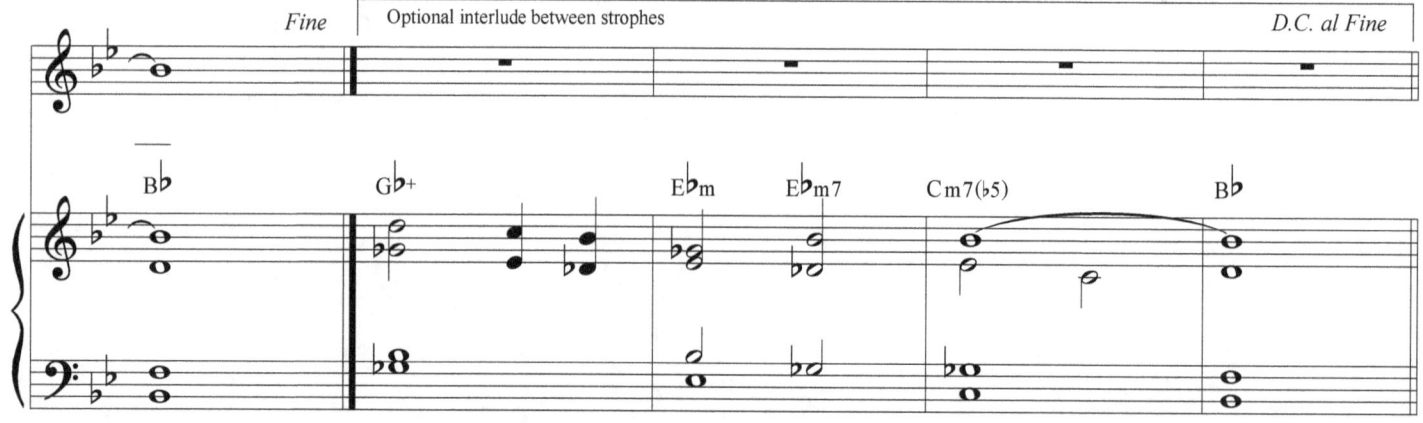

PSALM ONE
Eta (8.6.8.6.)

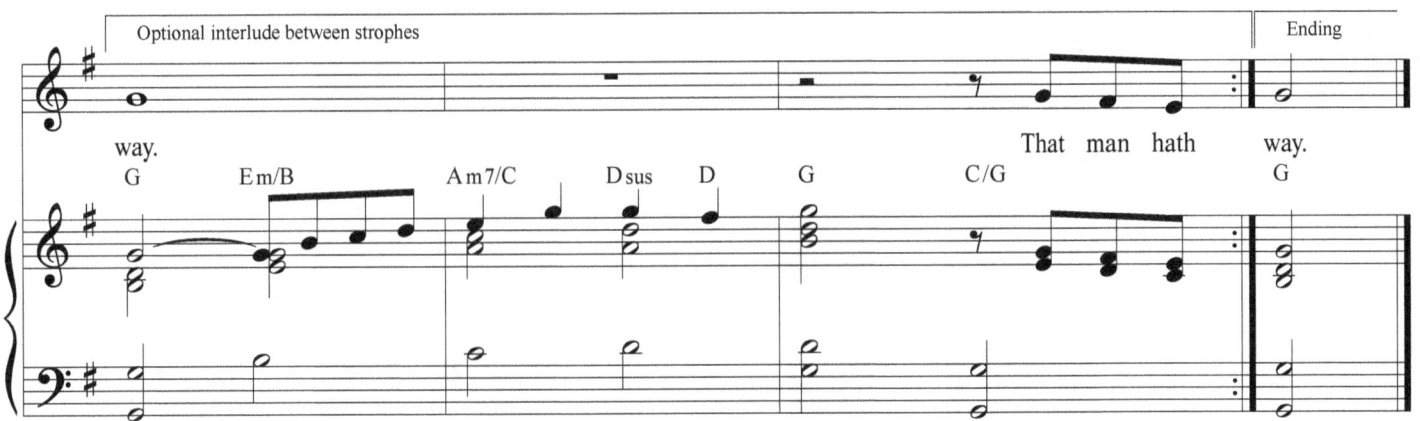

PSALM ONE
Theta (8.6.8.6.)

PSALM ONE
Iota (8.6.8.6.)

PSALM ONE
Kappa (8.6.8.6.)

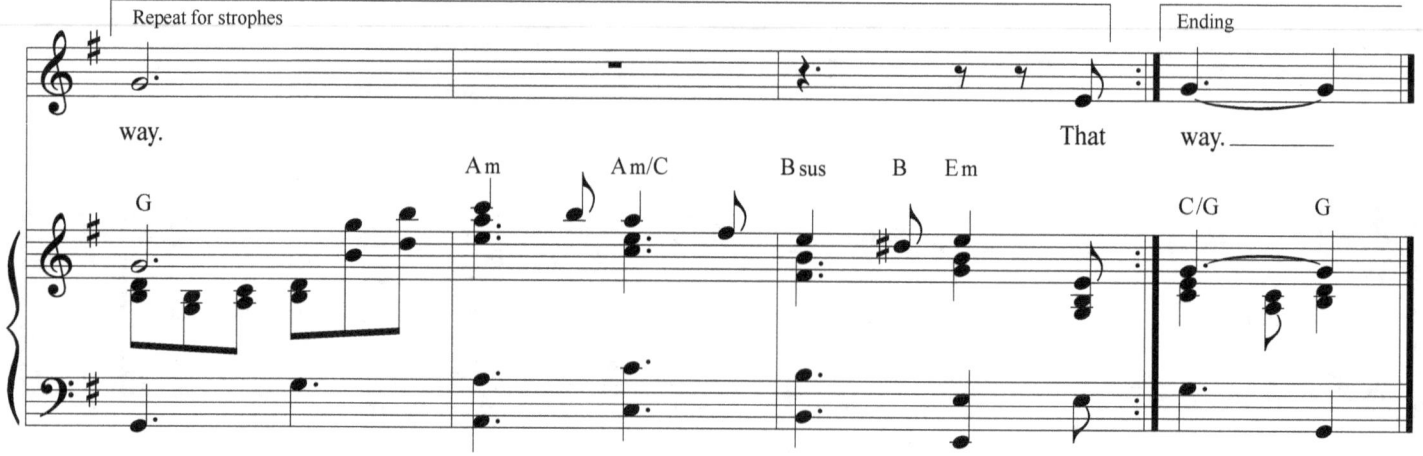

PSALM ONE
Lambda (8.6.8.6.)

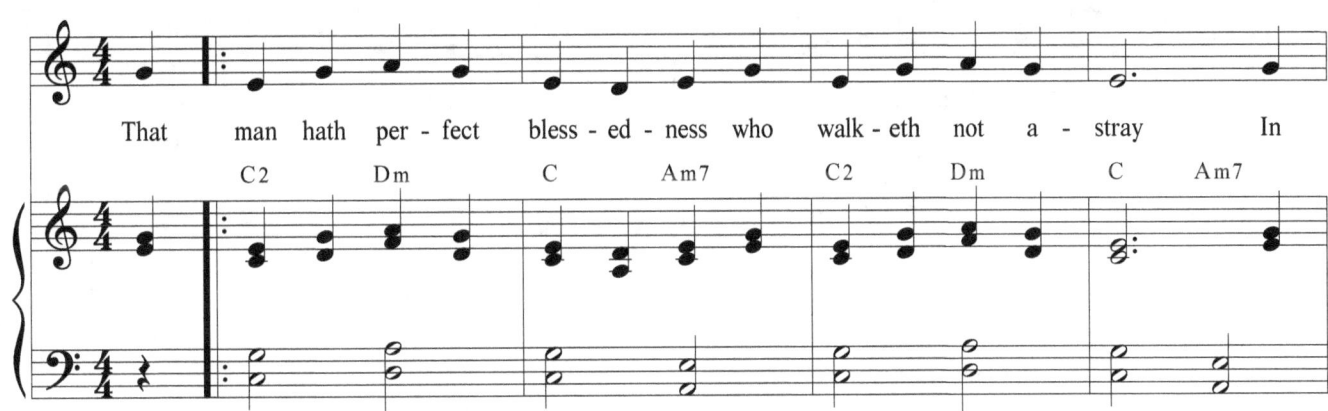

That man hath perfect bless-ed-ness who walk-eth not a-stray In

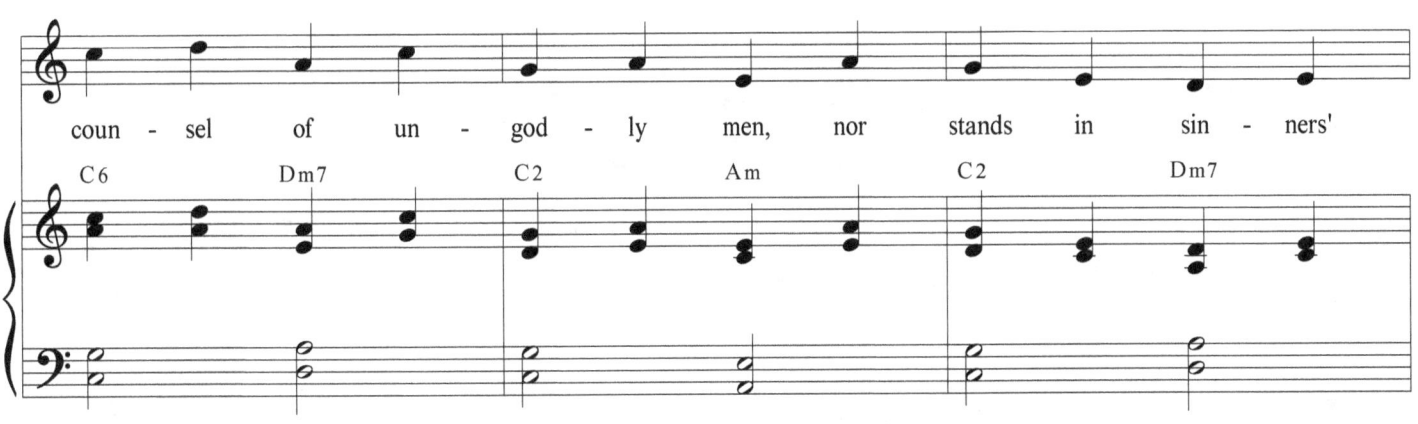

coun-sel of un-god-ly men, nor stands in sin-ners'

way   That man.

Optional interlde between strophes — *Ending*

PSALM ONE
Mu (8.6.8.6.D.)

PSALM ONE
Nu (8.6.8.6.D.)

PSALM ONE
Xi (8.6.8.6.D.)

PSALM ONE

Omicron (8.6.8.6.D.)

15

PSALM ONE
Rho (8.6.8.6.D.)

PSALM ONE
Sigma (8.6.8.6.D.)

PSALM ONE
Tau (8.6.8.6.D.)

PSALM ONE
Upsilon (8.6.8.6.D.)

PSALM ONE
Phi (8.6.8.6.D.)

PSALM ONE
Chi (8.6.8.6.D.)

PSALM ONE
Psi (8.6.8.6.D.)

PSALM ONE
Omega (8.6.8.6.D.)